# 50
**THINGS YOU SHOULD KNOW ABOUT** THE **HUMAN BODY**

## by Angela Royston

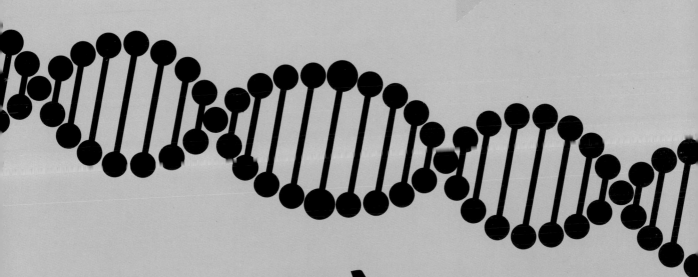

**Consultant:** Patricia Macnair
**Editors:** Carly Madden, Claudia Martin
**Designers:** Angela Ball and Dave Ball,
Mike Henson
**Illustrators:** Martin Foster, Sara Lynn Cramb
**Editorial Director:** Victoria Garrard
**Art Director:** Laura Roberts-Jensen
**Associate Publisher:** Maxime Boucknooghe
**Publisher:** Zeta Jones

Copyright © QED Publishing 2015

First published in the UK in 2015 by
QED Publishing
Part of The Quarto Group
The Old Brewery,
6 Blundell Street,
London, N7 9BH

www.qed-publishing.co.uk

A catalogue record for this book is available
from the British Library.

ISBN 978 1 78493 134 6

Printed in China

**Words in** CAPITALS **are explained
in the Glossary on page 78.**

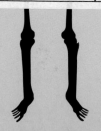

# CONTENTS

The human body is complicated and incredible! The many parts of the body form a network of systems that work together to keep you alive and active. Different systems allow you to move, be aware of what is happening around you, breathe, eat, transport food and oxygen around the body, get rid of waste, and produce babies.

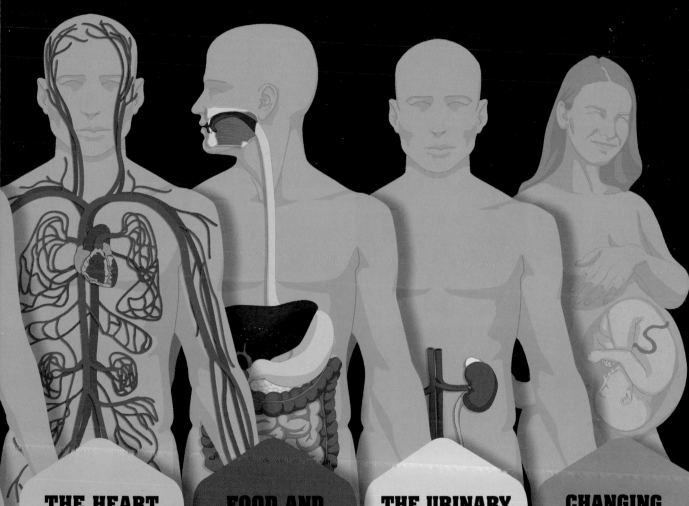

## THE HEART AND BLOOD

The heart, blood and BLOOD VESSELS make up the body's transport system. They carry oxygen, food and waste.

## FOOD AND DIGESTION

The digestive system breaks down food into NUTRIENTS that the body can use to stay alive and healthy.

## THE URINARY SYSTEM

Kidneys separate waste and excess water from blood, making URINE. Urine trickles down to the bladder.

## CHANGING BODIES

A baby develops from a single fertilized egg. Your body grows and changes throughout life.

A human person grows from one cell, which divides over and over again to form all the different parts of the body. Each part of the body is made of its own type of cell. For example, the heart is made of heart cells, the bones are made of bone cells, and your hair is made of hair cells.

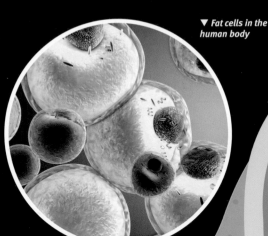
▼ Fat cells in the human body

## SIZE OF CELLS

CELLS are so small you need a magnifying glass or even a powerful microscope to see them. Some of the smallest cells are in the brain. They measure 0.004 millimetres, which means that more than 300 would fit across this full stop.

**Cytoplasm** is mostly water.

**Membrane** protects the cell.

▶ A human cell is made up of cytoplasm enclosed within a membrane. The organelles, such as the nucleus, float in the cytoplasm.

*The human body is made of 37,000,000,000,000 microscopic cells.*

## NEW CELLS FOR OLD

Your body is constantly making new cells. As you grow up, your body builds new cells to make you taller. But even when you are fully grown, your body makes millions of new cells every second of every day to replace those that have worn out or died. For example, cells in the lining of the INTESTINES live only a few days before they die and have to be replaced. Brain and heart cells, however, are almost never replaced – they last your whole life, so look after them!

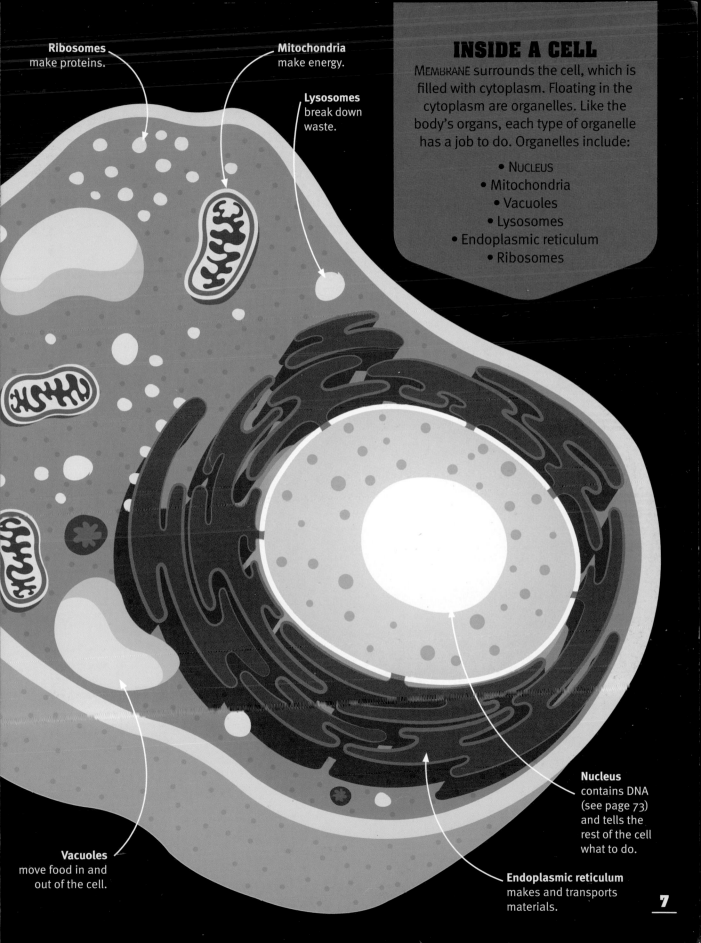

**Ribosomes**
make proteins.

**Mitochondria**
make energy.

**Lysosomes**
break down
waste.

# INSIDE A CELL

MEMBRANE surrounds the cell, which is
filled with cytoplasm. Floating in the
cytoplasm are organelles. Like the
body's organs, each type of organelle
has a job to do. Organelles include:

- NUCLEUS
- Mitochondria
- Vacuoles
- Lysosomes
- Endoplasmic reticulum
- Ribosomes

**Nucleus**
contains DNA
(see page 73)
and tells the
rest of the cell
what to do.

**Vacuoles**
move food in and
out of the cell.

**Endoplasmic reticulum**
makes and transports
materials.

# THE OUTER BODY

Skin is a thin, tough layer that covers most of your body. It protects your insides from the outside world.

It stops dirt, germs and other harmful things from getting into your body, except through your nose, mouth and other breaks in the skin.

Skin is like elastic – it bends and stretches as you move and then springs back into shape.

**HAIR** on your head grows the fastest (see page 12).

**THINNEST SKIN** is found on your eyelids, where it is 1–2 millimetres thick.

**SWEAT GLANDS** are found almost everywhere on the body, apart from the lips and ear canal. Sweat helps to keep you cool (see page 11).

## WET SUIT

Much of the inside of your body – such as the stomach and lungs – is covered with mucus, making it a bit slimy. It needs to stay that way! Skin is watertight to stop the moisture inside your body drying out.

**Skin is the boundary between your insides and the outside world.**

# Temperature control

Skin helps to keep your body at an even temperature. Your body is most comfortable at a temperature of about **37° Celsius**. If you become too cold, you shiver and your skin breaks out in goosebumps. If you become too hot, your sweat glands produce more sweat.

## TOO HOT

When you get too hot, your skin comes to your rescue. Sweat glands pump out more sweat. Salty liquid seeps from the pores onto the skin, where it cools you down as it slowly evaporates. At the same time, blood vessels expand, allowing more blood to reach the surface of the skin and cool.

▲ *Sweat glands ooze salty water.*

## TOO COLD

Shivering is caused by your muscles moving very fast. The movement makes heat, which is carried around the body in the blood. Goosebumps occur when tiny muscles at the root of the hairs on your skin make the hairs stand up. This traps air, which makes you warmer, like a bird fluffing its feathers.

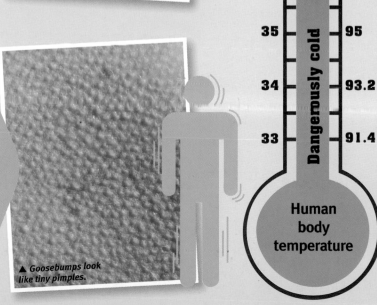

▲ *Goosebumps look like tiny pimples.*

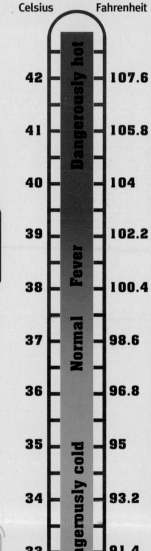

| Celsius | | Fahrenheit |
|---|---|---|
| 42 | Dangerously hot | 107.6 |
| 41 | | 105.8 |
| 40 | | 104 |
| 39 | Fever | 102.2 |
| 38 | | 100.4 |
| 37 | Normal | 98.6 |
| 36 | | 96.8 |
| 35 | | 95 |
| 34 | Dangerously cold | 93.2 |
| 33 | | 91.4 |

**Human body temperature**

# Hair raising

Fine hairs grow all over your skin, except on the palms of your hands, the soles of your feet, and your lips. Hair usually grows longest and thickest on your head, where it protects your scalp from the sun and keeps your head warm.

## BALDNESS

Many men slowly become bald as they get older. Some of their hair follicles stop working and their hair becomes thinner and disappears altogether on the top of their head. Other people may lose their hair due to a treatment for cancer or other medical condition. The hair grows back again afterwards.

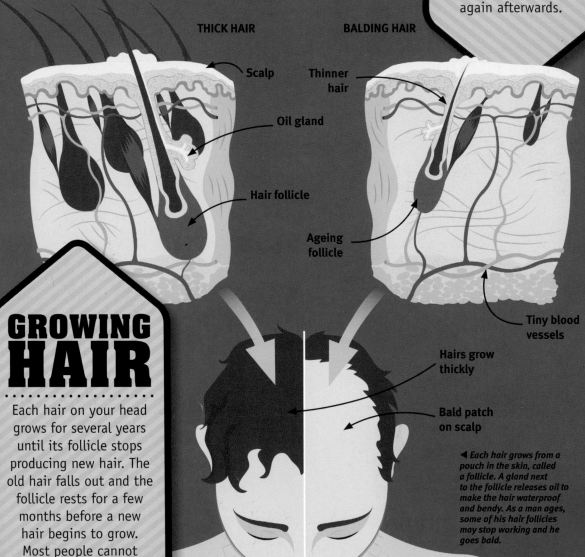

THICK HAIR

BALDING HAIR

Scalp

Thinner hair

Oil gland

Hair follicle

Ageing follicle

Tiny blood vessels

Hairs grow thickly

Bald patch on scalp

◀ Each hair grows from a pouch in the skin, called a follicle. A gland next to the follicle releases oil to make the hair waterproof and bendy. As a man ages, some of his hair follicles may stop working and he goes bald.

## GROWING HAIR

Each hair on your head grows for several years until its follicle stops producing new hair. The old hair falls out and the follicle rests for a few months before a new hair begins to grow. Most people cannot grow their hair for more than 1 metre before their hair follicles rest.

# Tough nails

Nails are hard plates, which protect the tips of the fingers and toes. Fingernails help you to pick up small objects, because they give the fingertips something to press against. They are also useful for scratching an itch!

▲ Nails feel smooth, but a microscope shows they are actually made of tiny flakes.

## HOW NAILS GROW

Fingernails grow about 2.5 millimetres a month. New nail cells grow below the cuticle, the thicker skin at the bottom of the nail. As the nail grows, the cells are pushed towards the tip. The longer the finger, the faster the nail grows, so the middle finger grows fastest and the little finger slowest.

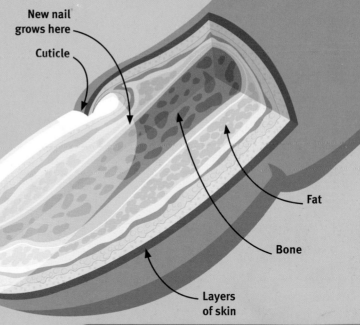

New nail grows here

Cuticle

Fat

Bone

Layers of skin

Nail

▲ The longest fingernail ever recorded measured 80 centimetres and belonged to Lee Redmond of the USA.

## CUTTING YOUR NAILS

If you didn't cut your nails, they would crack and break, so it is better to trim the white rim to keep it short and smooth. Nail is made of dead cells so cutting it does not hurt. Take care not to cut the pink part of the nail, however, because the skin below it will hurt.

A few people have managed to grow their nails more than 1 metre long!

# Spots and rashes

**Skin is tough but it is also sensitive. Sometimes it develops annoying pimples or becomes itchy. Some itches are caused by allergies or reactions to things in the environment. Eczema, for example, is when the skin becomes irritated, making it red, flaky, itchy and cracked.**

▼ *Eczema is most common on the elbows, knees, hands, neck, cheeks and scalp.*

## SPOTS

Acne is the most common cause of pimples and spots, particularly among teenagers. It usually occurs on the face, neck, upper back and chest. A spot forms when an oil gland in the skin becomes blocked and then infected by bacteria. Most outbreaks of acne can be easily treated with special anti-bacterial products.

# SKIN
## REACTIONS

Illnesses such as chicken pox and scarlet fever cause spots and rashes, but a rash can also be caused by an ALLERGY. This is when your body reacts to something that is harmless to most people. People who are allergic to cosmetics or eating strawberries, for example, may come out in a rash or in itchy bumps.

❶ Oil glands release oil into skin pores. Usually, it flows onto the skin surface. Sometimes a duct becomes blocked with dead cells.

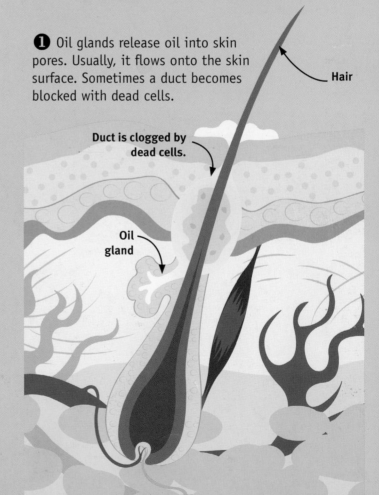

Hair

Duct is clogged by dead cells.

Oil gland

Athlete's foot is a FUNGUS that grows between the toes. It makes the skin itchy and flaky. Although it is called athlete's foot, anyone can catch it! Another skin infection caused by a fungus is ringworm. The fungus forms red rings on the skin that may be scaly and itchy. It's got nothing to do with worms!

## ITCHY HEAD

An itchy head can be caused by:

- **Dry or dirty hair or scalp.**
- **Dandruff:** when white flakes of dry skin fall out of your hair, often caused by a fungal infection.
- **Head lice:** insects that bite your scalp and lay eggs in your nice clean hair.

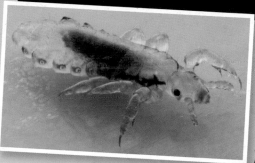

◀ Head louse clinging to human hair

**2** Oil starts to build up behind the blockage, making the gland swell up. Bacteria begin to multiply.

The skin starts to become inflamed.

Bacteria

The gland swells with oil.

A pustule, or spot, is formed.

**3** An inflamed pustule develops at the skin surface. The infected gland is swollen with pus.

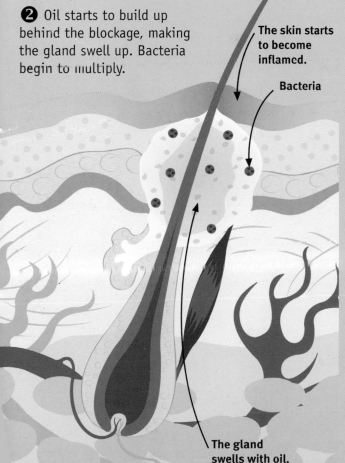

Infected gland is filled with pus.

# THE NERVOUS SYSTEM

The nervous system consists of the brain, the senses and the nerves. The senses collect information about the world. The information is changed into electrical signals, which are transmitted along the nerves to the brain, the body's control centre. But that is only half of the story. The nervous system also transmits signals from the brain along different nerves to the muscles and the glands.

**THE BRAIN**
is the body's control centre (see page 28).

**EARS**
react to sound to produce the sense of hearing (see page 20).

**EYES**
react to light to produce the sense of sight (see page 18).

**NOSE**
reacts to chemicals in the air to produce the sense of smell (see page 22).

**THE SPINAL CORD**
is a superhighway along which nerve signals travel to and from the brain.

**THE TONGUE**
reacts to chemicals in food to produce the sense of taste (see page 23).

are formed before you are born and they cannot be replaced.

**MOTOR NERVES** transmit signals from the brain to muscles and glands (see page 26).

# FIVE SENSES

The five senses are sight, hearing, smell, taste and touch. Each sense has its own sense organs, which react to different aspects of the environment. For example, we see because our eyes react to light. We can see shapes even in dim light.

The nervous system is a complex and efficient communication system.

**SENSORY NERVES** transmit signals from the senses to the brain (see page 26).

# NERVOUS SYSTEM FACTS

**BRAIN CELLS**

A few parts of the brain continue to grow new brain cells in the first two years after birth.

**HIDDEN EAR**

The part of the ear you see is only a small part of the whole ear. The rest is hidden inside your head.

**TWO EYES**

Having two eyes that focus on the same thing allows your brain to judge how far away the object is.

# How we see

We see because light enters our eyes. The light goes through the pupils, the dark hole at the centre of each eye. Most of the eye is hidden behind the pupil, but the whole eye is delicate and easily harmed. Much of the outer eye is designed to protect the inner eye.

## PROTECTING THE EYE

The eyelids close automatically whenever something comes dangerously close to the eye. The eye's surface is also protected by a transparent shield called the cornea. The cornea needs to be kept moist and this is also the job of the eyelids. Every time you blink, the eyelid washes the cornea with salty water.

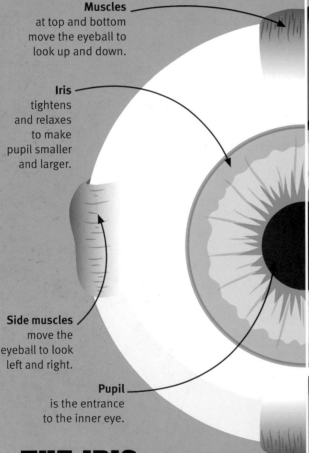

**Muscles** at top and bottom move the eyeball to look up and down.

**Iris** tightens and relaxes to make pupil smaller and larger.

**Side muscles** move the eyeball to look left and right.

**Pupil** is the entrance to the inner eye.

**Eyelid** closes to clean the surface of the eyeball.

**Eyelashes** help to stop dust getting into the eye.

## THE IRIS

The pupil is surrounded by a coloured ring, called the iris. The iris is a muscle which controls the size of the pupil. In dim light the pupil opens to let in more light, and in bright light it becomes smaller.

**You blink automatically every few seconds.**

# Seeing clearly

Inside the eye is a lens, which focuses the light to make a picture on a layer at the back of the eyeball called the retina. The picture, however, is upside down! The retina contains nerve cells, which send signals to the brain along the optic nerve. The brain then 'sees' the image correctly.

## SEEING COLOUR

The retina contains two types of cells – rods and cones. Rods detect light and dark, while cones detect colour. Cones only work in bright light, so in dim light we rely on the rods, which show things in shades of grey.

The retina contains about 126 million cells that react to light.

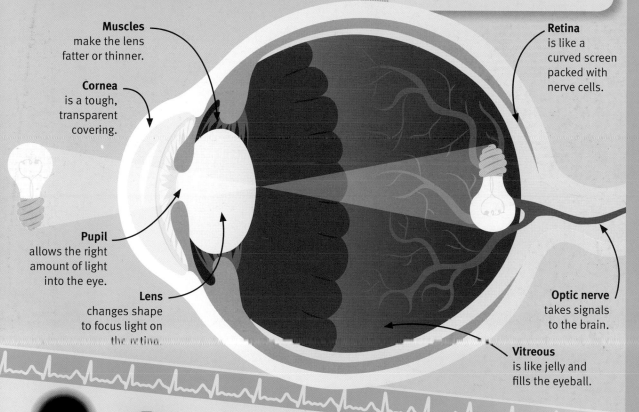

**Muscles**
make the lens fatter or thinner.

**Cornea**
is a tough, transparent covering.

**Pupil**
allows the right amount of light into the eye.

**Lens**
changes shape to focus light on the retina.

**Retina**
is like a curved screen packed with nerve cells.

**Optic nerve**
takes signals to the brain.

**Vitreous**
is like jelly and fills the eyeball.

## SHORT AND LONG SIGHT

Some people need glasses to help their eyes focus the light to give a clear picture on the retina. People with short sight have glasses that make things far away look clearer. People with long sight have glasses that make things close to them look clear.

**11**

# What is sound?

When something makes a sound it vibrates, making the air around it vibrate, too. The vibrations spread as sound waves in every direction, like ripples in a pond. You hear sound when some of the vibrations reach your ears.

## PASSING ON VIBRATIONS

Sound waves travel through solids and liquids as well as through the air. You can hear what is happening in another room because the sound waves make the walls VIBRATE. The vibrations pass through the wall and make the air on the other side vibrate, too. They then travel through the air to your ears.

◄ Very loud sounds can damage your ears. People who play in a band often use special headphones to protect their ears.

## COLLECTING THE SOUND

Your outer ear collects the sound and directs it down your ear canal to a thin layer of skin called the eardrum. Earwax is a thick, yellow substance that helps keep your ear canal clear so that sound can reach the eardrum. Earwax catches dirt and pushes it out of your ear.

# Listen up!

The eardrum vibrates like the surface of a drum. The movement is picked up and magnified by three small bones in the middle ear. Vibrations then pass into the cochlea in the inner ear. Liquid inside the cochlea carries the sound waves to special cells that send signals along nerves to the brain.

## SELECT SOUNDS

The brain is fantastically good at filtering out unimportant background sounds. You may notice when a plane goes overhead, but hardly hear the constant sound of traffic outside.

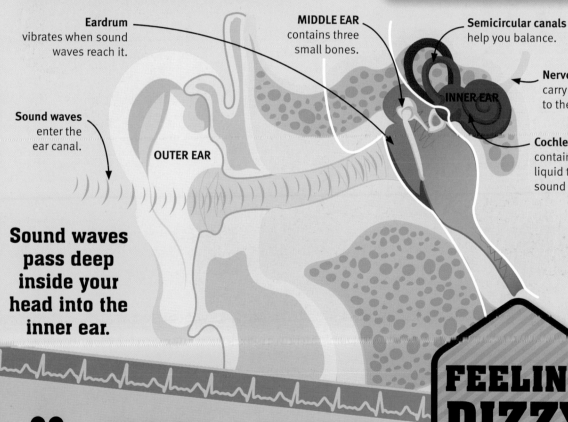

**Eardrum** vibrates when sound waves reach it.

**MIDDLE EAR** contains three small bones.

**Semicircular canals** help you balance.

**Nerves** carry signals to the brain.

**Sound waves** enter the ear canal.

**OUTER EAR**

INNER EAR

**Cochlea** contains liquid to carry sound waves.

**Sound waves pass deep inside your head into the inner ear.**

## KEEPING A BALANCE

Just part of the inner ear is involved in hearing. The other part, called the SEMICIRCULAR CANALS, is essential for balance. The canals are filled with liquid and so, as you move, the liquid also moves and tells your brain which way up you are.

## FEELING DIZZY

If you spin round and then stop, you may feel dizzy. This is because the liquid in your inner ears is still moving around!

When you are asleep, your ears still hear – but your brain ignores most noises.

# What a smell!

You hold your nose if you want to block out a nasty smell, but you sniff hard if you want to smell something better. That is because the cells that detect smells are at the top of the inside of your nose.

## REACTING TO SMELLS

The inside of the nose is lined with mucus. The smell cells only detect chemicals that are dissolved in the mucus. When smell signals reach the brain, the body may react in different ways. A delicious food smell may make your mouth water, but a disgusting smell may make you feel sick.

**Brain**
receives signals about smell from the olfactory bulb.

**Olfactory bulb**
is the smell sense organ. It collects signals from the smell cells and passes them along nerves to the brain.

**Smell cells**
are packed together high up in the passages of the nose.

**Chemicals**
which you detect as smells enter your nose when you breathe in.

## SMELLY CHEMICALS

You smell things when chemicals in the air reach your nose. Some things, like coffee, have a strong smell, because lots of tiny particles of coffee escape into the air. Other things, such as glass, have no smell, because they do not release chemicals.

## BASIC TASTES

There are four basic tastes – sweet, salty, sour and bitter. All tastes are made up of these. Scientists have recently discovered a fifth basic taste called savoury or umami, which is a sort of meaty taste.

Special taste cells in your mouth react to chemicals in food. Taste cells are hidden inside taste buds and most of them are on your tongue. Taste and smell are closely linked. It's much harder to taste if your nose is blocked and you cannot smell.

**SAVOURY**

**SOUR**

**BITTER**

**SALTY**

**SWEET**

▼ *Taste buds up close*

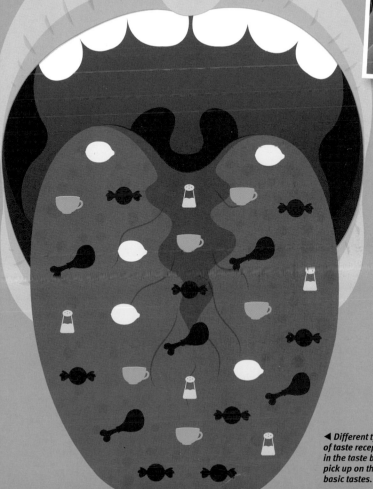

◀ *Different types of taste receptors in the taste buds pick up on the five basic tastes.*

## GETTING THE TASTE

❶ Chemicals in food and drink dissolve in SALIVA in the mouth.

❷ Saliva gets inside a taste bud, which contains 50 to 150 taste cells.

❸ Taste cells send messages to the brain.

❹ At the same time, smell cells send messages to the brain about the smell.

❺ The combination of taste and smell gives the full taste.

Taste cells last only for 1 to 2 weeks before they die and are replaced.

# Touch and feel

The sense of touch is not so much one sense as several. Different types of nerve cells, called TOUCH RECEPTORS, respond to touch, pain and temperature. Most touch receptors are in the skin, but receptors in the muscles, stomach and other parts of the body keep us informed of what is going on inside our bodies, too.

Surface of skin

## WHAT YOU FEEL

Nerve endings around the hair roots pick up the slightest movement of fine hairs on your skin, making you instantly aware of anything that touches you. However, different kinds of nerve endings in the skin react to:

 itches and tickles

 pressure and heavier touch

heat and cold

pain

Merkel nerve endings react to pressure and are common in the fingertips.

**FINGERTIPS**

The fingertips are one of the most SENSITIVE areas of your skin. They are packed with nerve endings, which allow you to feel tiny bumps and variations in a surface which you probably cannot even see.

Sweat gland

**Skin has about 5 million touch receptors, which send signals to the brain.**

**Tactile nerve endings**
near the surface of
the skin react fast to
light touch but soon
switch off.

*▼ Different types
of nerve endings in
the skin respond
to different types
of touch.*

Epidermis

Dermis

**Free nerve endings**
react to pain, itch
and temperature.

**Ruffini nerve endings**
in the dermis react
to bending and stretching
in the skin.

**Pacinian endings**
deep in the skin react
to pressure and to
vibrations up to
5 centimetres away.

# INCREASING PRESSURE

Different types of nerve endings react to
different levels of touch. The lightest
touch is experienced as soft and even
tickly. Heavier touch is felt as pressure
and perhaps squeezing or stretching.
When touch becomes uncomfortable or
damaging, you feel it as increasing pain.
Pain is unpleasant but it is the body's way
of telling you that something is wrong.

*▶ Here the
areas of the
body that are
sensitive to
touch are
shown larger.*

# SENSITIVE
# AREAS

Different parts of
the body are more
sensitive to touch and
to changes in
temperature. The
lips and tongue are very
sensitive to both. Your
back, however, is one of
the areas least sensitive
to touch. The elbow
is sensitive to heat,
because it has lots
of nerve endings that
react to temperature.

# High-speed nerves

There are two kinds of nerves. Sensory nerves transmit signals from the eyes, ears and other sense organs to the brain. Motor nerves carry instructions from the brain or spinal cord to the muscles and glands. A nerve consists of a bundle of nerve cells, called neurons, that link together to pass on electrical signals.

## SUPER HIGHWAY OF NERVES

Most sensory and motor nerves go through the spinal cord from and to all parts of the body. The longest nerve cells are over 1 metre long. These are motor NEURONS in the spine that help to transmit signals to muscles in the feet.

Nerve signals travel up to 100 metres (the length of a football pitch) per second!

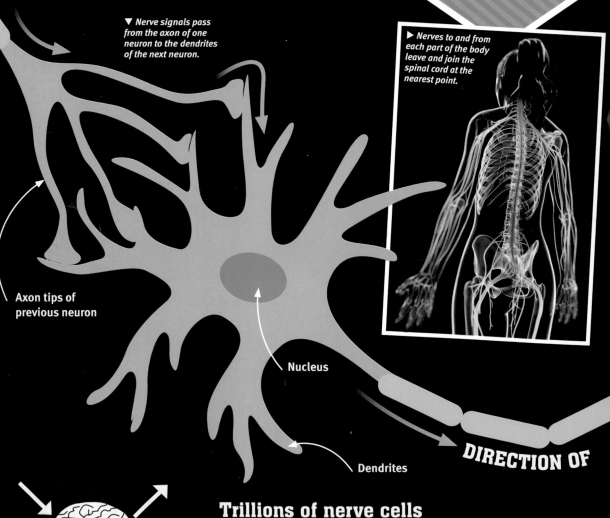

▼ Nerve signals pass from the axon of one neuron to the dendrites of the next neuron.

▶ Nerves to and from each part of the body leave and join the spinal cord at the nearest point.

Axon tips of previous neuron

Nucleus

Dendrites

DIRECTION OF

Trillions of nerve cells carry messages to and from the brain.

When the brain receives messages from the senses it may respond by triggering particular muscles. For example:

| SENSORY NERVES CARRY SIGNALS TO BRAIN |  | MOTOR NERVES TAKE INSTRUCTIONS FROM BRAIN |
|---|---|---|
| from eyes while playing computer game | → | to muscles that move fingers |
| *from tongue that something tastes bad* | → | *to muscles in mouth to spit* |
| from ears that phone is ringing | → | to muscles in arms to pick up phone |

# FAST REACTIONS

In an emergency, a message is passed from the sensory nerves directly through the spinal cord to the motor nerves. This is a reflex. For example, if you touch something hot, you pull your hand away before your brain registers the pain.

**ELECTRICAL SIGNAL**

Nucleus

Dendrites of next neuron

Axon tips

**AUTOMATIC PATHWAY**

If you often repeat a particular action in response to a message from the senses, the action will become automatic – you will do it without thinking. This is why sportspeople practise their skills over and over again!

▲ *The more often you play a sport, the more you perform the skills automatically.*

# Brilliant brain

**The brain is a soft, pinky-grey organ, which controls everything you do, from breathing to reading to working out difficult maths questions. It also stores memories and feelings.**

## COMMUNICATION PATHWAYS

The brain receives information from the senses and sends signals to the rest of the body. The brain also communicates with itself! The billions of neurons that make up the brain form pathways, which communicate with each other.

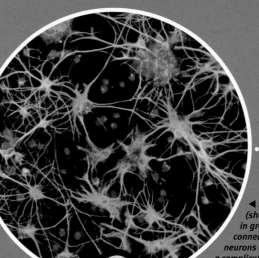

◄ *Neurons (shown here in green) connect to other neurons to form a complicated network in the brain.*

Concentration, planning and problem-solving

**FRONTAL LOBE**
helps to control thinking, movement and behaviour.

**TEMPORAL LOBE**
helps to control speech, memory and smell.

Facial recognition

## LEARNING

When you learn something new, your brain links neurons to form a new pathway. Suppose you are learning to play the recorder. At first, you struggle. Soon you can play almost without thinking, because connections have been made between the neurons involved.

▲ *Everything you are aware of happens in the four lobes of the cerebral cortex.*

**The brain contains 100 billion neurons, or nerve cells, closely packed together.**

# LOBES OF THE CORTEX

The four LOBES are related to different brain functions. Some functions are shared between lobes.

# Incredible cortex

The cerebral cortex is the wrinkled and folded outer layer of the brain. It is the conscious part of the brain. Its four areas, called lobes, allow us to think and react to the evidence of our senses.

The human cortex is bigger and more complex than that of any other animal.

Touch and pressure

Taste

Body awareness

**PARIETAL LOBE** helps to make sense of information from the senses.

Understanding words

**OCCIPITAL LOBE** helps to control sight.

**CEREBELLUM** helps to control balance and movement.

Coordination

**Brainstem** controls heartbeat, breathing and other functions. It monitors and coordinates the messages that enter and leave the brain.

## HIDDEN BRAIN

We are only aware of what happens in our cortex. The rest of the brain, including the cerebellum and brainstem, controls what is automatic or unconscious, such as the action of the heart, the kidneys and so on.

## ASLEEP OR AWAKE?

Only the cortex sleeps. The rest of the brain never stops working. Parts of the cortex are busy, too, even when we are asleep. Dreams, for example, are probably a mixture of thoughts and events that happened during the day, mixed with fears and memories.

# BONES AND MUSCLES

Bones are the rigid, hard parts inside your body. They fit together to form your skeleton. This supports and protects your organs and gives your body its basic shape. Muscles are soft and fleshy. They make the bones move and cover most of your body to give it its outward, rounded shape.

**THE SKULL** is the bone that forms your head and protects your brain.

**RIBS** curve round to form a cage that protects your heart and lungs.

**THE SPINE** is made up of 26 knobbly bones called vertebrae.

**MUSCLES** move parts of the body, particularly the bones, but also the tongue and face. Muscles often work in pairs (see page 36).

An adult has 206 bones and more than 600 muscles.

**THE FEMUR** is the thigh bone and is the longest bone in the body.

**A JOINT** is where two bones meet and fit together (see page 34).

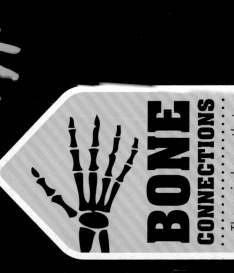

# BONE CONNECTIONS

The main bones that shape the human body are the spine, the legs and arms, the ribs, the pelvis and the skull. Most bones are linked directly or indirectly to the spine. For example, the upper arm bone joins the shoulder blade, which joins to the spine. The lower arm bones and the bones of the wrist and hands link to the upper arm bones.

## BONE & MUSCLE FACTS

**STRONG BITE**

The masseter muscle is the strongest muscle in the body. It shuts your mouth when you bite.

**SMALLEST BONE**

The smallest bone is the stirrup-shaped stapes in your middle ear. It is smaller than a grain of rice!

**BABY BONES**

A baby has about 300 bones when it is born. Many of these bones join together as a child grows.

**FLEXIBLE SHOULDER**

The shoulder joint has a greater range of movement than any other joint. It can move in every direction.

# Bare bones

Bones are hard and strong. They are the framework that supports the heart, stomach and other vital organs. If bones were completely solid, they would be very heavy to move, so the inside of bones consists of lightweight crisscross struts.

▼ *Your two hands and wrists contain 54 bones altogether.*

**Phalange bones** make up the fingers.

## FROM BENDY TO RIGID

Bone growth takes place in a layer of CARTILAGE near the end of the bone, called the epiphyseal plate. Cartilage is strong but bendy. New cartilage is formed in the epiphyseal plate. Slowly the cartilage hardens into bone, which contains calcium and other minerals to make it rigid. Your bones go on growing until you are about 25 years old.

Spongy bone

Compact bone

Bone cavity contains marrow.

## BONE LAYERS

The outer layer of a bone is solid and compact. Below the compact bone is a lighter, spongy bone. It is strong but it can absorb knocks and bangs. Some bones have a hollow centre, which is filled with a substance called bone marrow.

# INSIDE A BONE

The tiny gaps in spongy bone are filled with blood vessels. The blood feeds the bone and keeps it alive. At the same time, new blood cells (see page 50) are made in the bone marrow at the centre of many bones.

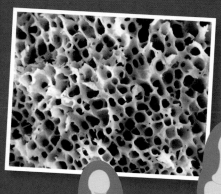

◄ Spongy bone is softer and more flexible than compact bone.

## SUIT OF ARMOUR

Some bones form a protective armour under your skin.

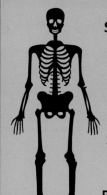

**SKULL** ➤ protects the brain, eyes and inner ears

**RIBS** ➤ protect the lungs, heart and liver

**SPINE** ➤ protects nerves in the spinal column

**PELVIS** ➤ protects the digestive organs

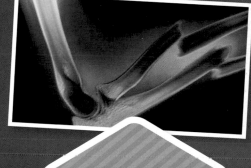

Metacarpals form the hands.

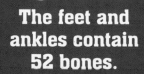

**The feet and ankles contain 52 bones.**

# MEND BROKEN BONES

A cracked or broken bone can mend itself, although a hard plaster cast may be used to keep it in position as it heals. After a bone is injured:

❶ Bone marrow and blood ooze from the bone into the crack.

❷ New bone slowly grows across the gap.

❸ Once the gap is filled, the new bone hardens into strong bone.

# Jiggle those joints

Joints allow bones to move, but not too much! Different-shaped joints allow different kinds of movement. Ball and socket joints at the shoulders give a wide circle of movement. Hinge joints at the knees allow movement in only one direction. Fixed joints allow no movement at all!

## BALL AND SOCKET JOINTS

Hips and shoulders are ball and socket JOINTS. The rounded top of the thigh bone, for example, fits into a hollow cup in the pelvis. It allows you to swing and circle your leg.

*Muscles help move joints* ▶
*(see pages 36–37)*

## GLIDING JOINT

Wrists and ankles have gliding joints, in which two flat bones can slide across each other.

## HINGE JOINTS

Knees and fingers are hinge joints. They can only bend and straighten.

## PIVOT JOINT

The neck is a pivot joint. A bone in the top vertebra passes through a hole at the bottom of the skull. This joint allows you to move your head from side to side.

## SADDLE JOINT

The base of the thumb is a saddle joint. It can hinge and slide in any direction. This means you can use your thumb and fingers to hold things.

◀ *There are 360 joints in the human body. Some joints allow us to move, while others – such as the joints in the skull – are fixed.*

## INSIDE A JOINT

Most joints contain a liquid called synovial fluid, which acts like oil to stop the ends of the bones rubbing together. It also helps the joint move more smoothly. LIGAMENTS are strong, bendy straps of TISSUE that stretch across the joint and bind it together. If a joint is pulled too far, the ligament may tear, causing a painful sprain.

Bone marrow

Spongy bone

Compact bone

Joint cavity contains synovial fluid.

Ligament

Cartilage

**35**

# Muscle power

You need the power of muscles to move any part of your body. Muscles in your face allow you to smile, frown and speak, but the largest muscles are attached to bones. Muscles pull, not push, so they often work in pairs – one to bend a bone over a joint and another to straighten it.

**The gluteus maximus in the buttocks is the largest muscle in the body.**

**Triceps** straightens the elbow.

**Gluteus maximus** helps to keep the body upright.

To straighten your arm, you tighten the triceps and relax the biceps.

To bend your arm, you tighten the biceps and relax the triceps.

**Biceps** bulges as it contracts.

**Biceps**

**Triceps**

**Triceps** becomes firmer as it contracts.

**Hamstring** bends the knee.

## HOW A MUSCLE WORKS

Muscles are made of bundles of FIBRES, which contract by becoming shorter and fatter. The fibres contract when the muscle receives a signal through the motor nerve. A muscle is attached to the bone it moves by a strap of strong tissue called a TENDON. When the muscle contracts, the tendon pulls the bone.

▲ Basketball players use muscles in their arms and legs to control the ball, to move and to stay steady on their feet.

# MUSCLES AND JOINTS

Muscles move a bone by contracting and pulling the bone around the joint. This means that the muscles that move your lower leg, for example, make you bend or straighten your knee. They are attached to your thigh bone, but the tendons reach across the knee joint to pull the bones in your lower leg.

**Deltoid** lifts the arms up or out to the side.

**Biceps** bends the elbow.

**Quadriceps** straightens the knee.

**Calf** flexes the foot around the ankle.

## MAKING MUSCLES BIGGER

If you use a muscle regularly, it works better and more efficiently. Exercise makes the fibres bigger and stronger, so that when they contract they produce more power. The thicker fibres make the muscle look bigger when it contracts.

# Getting fitter

Exercise involves using your bones, joints and muscles, but it makes your whole body work and feel better. The main types of exercise are aerobic (it makes you puff and pant!), flexibility (it exercises the joints) and exercises that make your muscles and bones stronger.

## STRONG MUSCLES

Activities such as climbing, cycling and swimming make you stronger and fitter, because they work your muscles hard. In cycling, for example, the muscles in your legs work hard to keep the pedals turning.

**Strong legs** help to balance.

**Quads** are used for pedalling.

**Calf muscles** help to turn pedals.

**Strong shoulders** support the body.

## BEND AND STRETCH

Gymnastics, ballet, break dancing, tai chi and yoga are five activities that strengthen your joints and muscles and help you to become more flexible. They make your tendons and ligaments stronger and more bendy so that you can control and move your joints better.

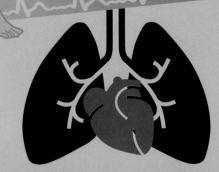

## STRONG BONES

Exercises such as jumping, running, gymnastics and tennis can strengthen the bones. As your weight hits the ground or hits a moving ball, your bones absorb the shock. This encourages the bones to make extra cells to strengthen the bone.

**Elbow joint**
bends and straightens as racket hits ball.

**Knee joint**
bends and straightens to change speed and direction.

**Ankle joint**
helps to balance.

## AEROBIC WORKOUT

AEROBIC EXERCISE includes running, cycling, swimming, dancing and any activity that makes you breathe deeper and your heart beat faster. This type of exercise makes your heart and lungs work better (see page 45) and improves your stamina so that you will be able to keep active for longer, before stopping to catch your breath!

### MUSCLE FUEL

Muscles are like engines, which burn fuel to produce movement. The fuel is carbohydrate from food (see page 54), but you also need oxygen to change the food into energy. Blood supplies the muscles with food and oxygen (see page 46).

# THE BREATHING SYSTEM

The breathing system consists of the nose, the mouth, the throat, the trachea (windpipe), the lungs and a muscle called the diaphragm. The system brings air into your lungs, where oxygen gas moves into your blood, and the waste gas – carbon dioxide – passes out of it.

**NOSE**
and mouth inhale and expel air (see page 42).

**TRACHEA**
joins the throat to the lungs (see page 43).

**BRONCHIAL TUBES**
divide into narrower tubes, which take air deep into the lungs (see page 43).

**INSIDE THE LUNGS**
the airways become even narrower and end in tiny AIR SACS (see page 45).

**LARYNX**
contains the vocal cords, which use out-breaths to make sounds.

**DIAPHRAGM**
is the muscle that makes you breathe air in and out of the lungs.

## HICCUPS

Sometimes the diaphragm twitches. With each jerk, you gulp in a breath of air and make the 'hic' sound. Hiccups can occur for no obvious reason, but sometimes they are triggered by swallowing before chewing a mouthful properly, or by eating particular foods.

**You breathe in and out about 20,000 times a day.**

## VOCAL CORDS

The larynx, or voice box, contains two vocal cords, which can vibrate as air passes out between them. The larynx makes a sound, but you have to move your lips, tongue and teeth to make all the sounds you need to speak.

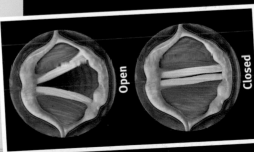

Open

Closed

▶ The vocal cords are open when you breathe in, and closed when you hold your breath. They vibrate when you are talking or singing.

## BREATHING FACTS

### TWO LUNGS

The right lung is slightly bigger than the left lung. The smaller left lung provides room for the heart.

### LARGE LUNG SURFACE

If opened out flat, the airways and air sacs inside the lungs would almost cover a tennis court!

### LOW OR SQUEAKY

The vocal cords open wide to make low sounds. Pulling them tight together produces a high squeak.

### PAUSING FOR BREATH

You can only talk as you breathe out, so every so often you have to stop talking and take a breath!

# In through the nose

The nose is much more than a passageway for air to get into the lungs. It helps to clean the air you breathe in and make it ready for your lungs. You can also breathe in through your mouth, which is essential for times when your nose is blocked!

## INSIDE THE NOSE

❶ Air moves into airways in the nose. The airways contain mucus, which warms the air and makes it moister.

❷ Tiny hair-like structures called cilia line the inside of the nose. They trap dirt, germs and other particles. Cilia move the particles back down the nostrils.

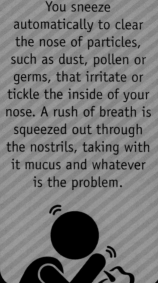

## ACHOO!

You sneeze automatically to clear the nose of particles, such as dust, pollen or germs, that irritate or tickle the inside of your nose. A rush of breath is squeezed out through the nostrils, taking with it mucus and whatever is the problem.

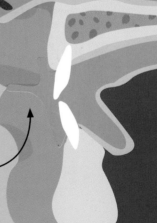

Airways

AIR

Mouth
can take in air when needed.

▲ Cilia inside the nose: here they have trapped bacteria (in yellow).

Sneezing pushes air out of your nose at up to 160 kilometres an hour!

# Down the tubes

Air passes from the nose or mouth into the throat. Food and drink also go down the throat and so the throat divides into two tubes. The trachea (windpipe) takes air to the lungs. The oesophagus (food pipe) takes food and liquid to the stomach.

▼ The trachea takes air to the lungs. The oesophagus takes food and liquid to the stomach.

**Air flows in** through the nose or mouth.

**Oesophagus** transports food to the stomach.

**Epiglottis** is a flap that closes the trachea when you swallow food and drink.

**Bronchioles**

**Trachea** takes air to the lungs.

## BRANCHING TUBES

The breathing tubes are like a tree with the TRACHEA as the trunk. The trachea divides into two main branches called bronchi, one for each lung. Each bronchi then divides into narrower tubes, called BRONCHIOLES. They are like the twigs on a tree.

To the stomach

Lung

Stomach

### COUGH COUGH

The BRONCHIAL TUBES are lined with mucus and tiny hairs, which catch any particles that manage to get through the nose. Sometimes bronchial tubes become blocked with thick mucus. Coughing pushes a blast of air through the tubes to clear them.

You choke when food or drink goes down the trachea.

43

# Air-filled lungs

Lungs are the second largest organs in the body, after the skin. They take up most of the space in your chest. They are filled with air. Each lung has about 400 million air sacs. The lungs only partly empty and fill with each breath but that brings in enough air to provide the body with the oxygen it needs.

## GASPING FOR BREATH

When you run fast or for a long time, your muscles are working hard. This means that they need lots of extra oxygen to keep going. The only way for the body to supply it is to take in extra air by breathing deeper and faster.

## THE INS AND OUTS

 **500 millilitres**
The volume of each breath when resting.

 **350 millilitres**
The amount of air that reaches air sacs.

**3 litres**
The deepest breath.

 **6 litres**
Total volume of lungs.

Running flat out makes you take in about 15 times more air than usual.

## IN AND OUT

Breathing is controlled by a sheet of muscle below the lungs called the diaphragm, and is helped by the ribs. The diaphragm moves down as it contracts and the ribs move out, making extra space in the lungs. Air is pulled in to fill the space. When the ribs and diaphragm relax, air is pushed out.

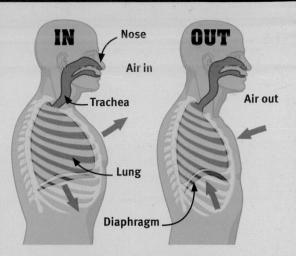

**IN**

Nose

Air in

Trachea

Lung

Diaphragm

**OUT**

Air out

**Bronchioles**

▼ Air sacs are in bunches at the ends of the bronchioles.

## GAS EXCHANGE

The bronchioles end in bunches of tiny air sacs, called alveoli. Each air sac is wrapped around with narrow blood vessels, called CAPILLARIES (see page 47). The walls of the air sacs and the capillaries are so thin that, when you breathe in, oxygen and carbon dioxide move easily from one to the other.

◄ The lungs take up most of the room inside the chest. They are the only part of the body that is lighter than water.

**Diaphragm**

tubes, called blood vessels, carry blood all around the body.

# 28 THE HEART AND BLOOD

**The heart, blood and blood vessels form an amazing transport system called the circulatory system. Blood collects oxygen from the lungs and food from the digestive system, and delivers them to every cell in your body. It also collects waste produced by the cells. The system is powered by an incredible pump – the heart.**

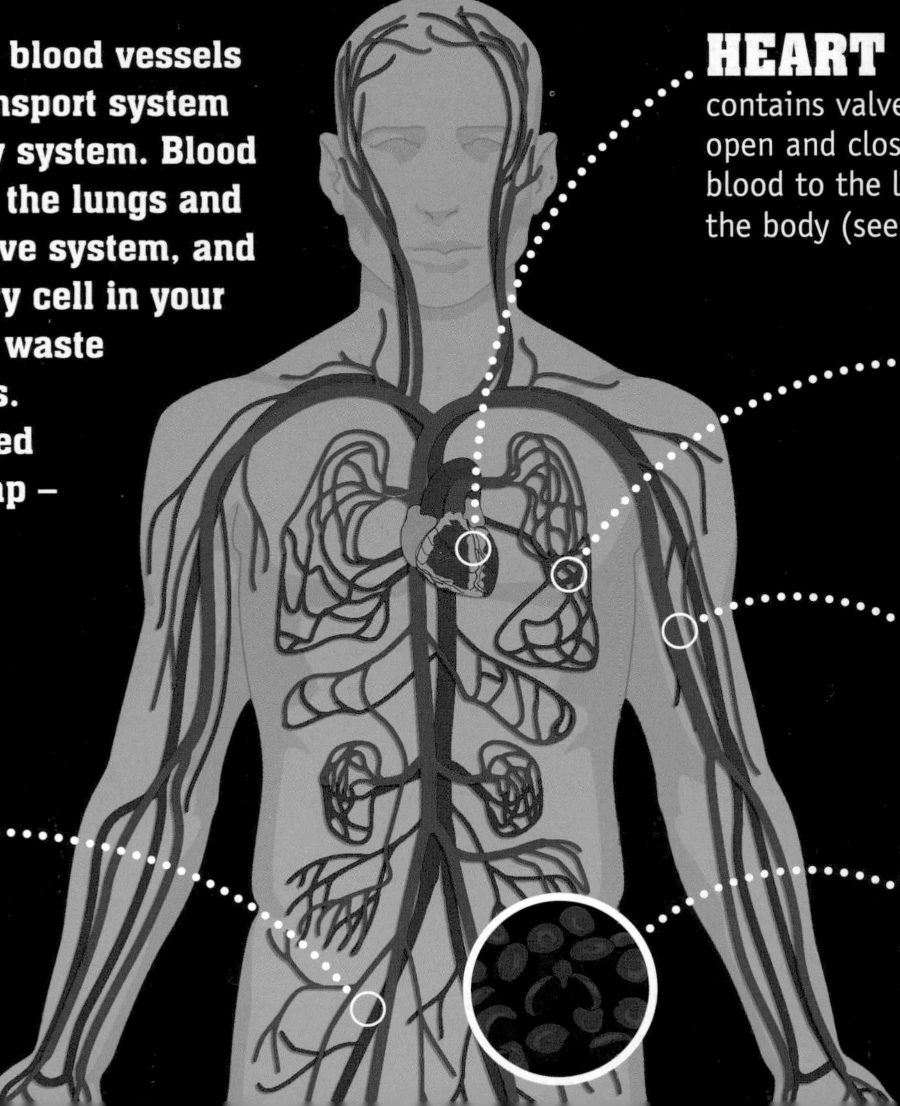

**HEART**
contains valves which open and close to send blood to the lungs or the body (see page 48).

**LUNGS**
are where blood picks up oxygen. The blood then returns to the heart.

**VEINS**
(shown here in blue) bring blood back to the heart.

**ARTERIES**
(shown here in red) take blood away from the heart.

**BLOOD**
consists of different types of cells floating in a salty liquid called plasma (see page 50).

▼ Red blood cells carry oxygen and give blood its red colour.

## CAPILLARIES

are narrow blood vessels which take blood to and from every cell.

If all the capillaries in a human body were laid end to end, they would stretch two and a half times around the world.

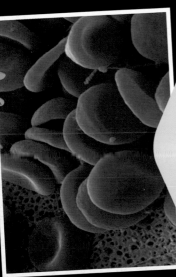

## CONSTANT CIRCULATION

Blood is pumped by the heart through the arteries, which branch into narrower and narrower capillaries. Blood then returns to the heart through capillaries and VEINS. Different arteries take blood to different parts of the body, but every blood cell probably passes through the heart about 1000 times a day.

## HEART & BLOOD FACTS

### BIG HEART
Your heart is about the same size as your clenched fist – it grows as you grow.

### WIDEST ARTERY
The widest ARTERY is the aorta, which takes blood carrying oxygen from the heart to the rest of the body.

### TINY CAPILLARIES
The narrowest capillaries are thinner than a single hair. Their walls are only one or two cells thick.

### SALTY PLASMA
Blood cells float in plasma, which is mostly water – along with carbon dioxide, salts and hormones.

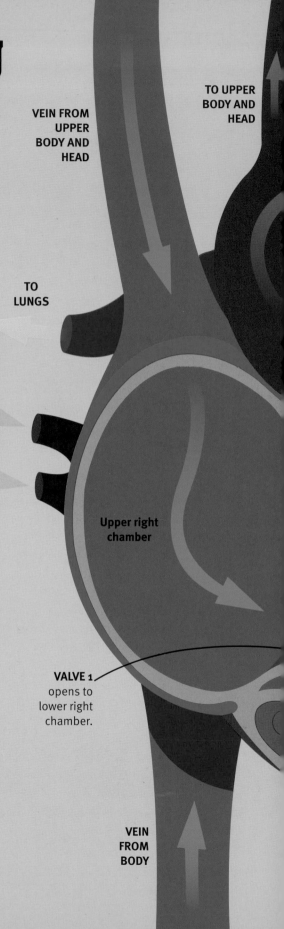

# Pounding heart

The heart is a muscle which contracts to pump blood into the arteries. The heart is in fact two pumps. The right side of the heart sends blood to the lungs. The left side pumps blood stocked with oxygen around the body.

**VEIN FROM UPPER BODY AND HEAD**

**TO UPPER BODY AND HEAD**

**TO LUNGS**

**FROM LUNGS**

**Upper right chamber**

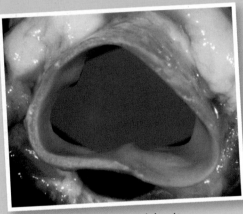

▲ Valves inside the heart open and close to keep blood flowing in the correct direction.

## HEART VALVES

Four VALVES control the direction blood flows through the heart. Blood from the body enters the upper right chamber.

• **Valve 1** allows blood to flow from the upper right to the lower right chamber.

• **Valve 2** opens so blood flows from the lower right chamber to the lungs. Blood returns from the lungs into the upper left chamber.

• **Valve 3** allows blood to flow from the upper left to the lower left chamber.

• **Valve 4** opens to let oxygen-rich blood flow from the lower left chamber to the body.

**VALVE 1** opens to lower right chamber.

**VEIN FROM BODY**

**Blood flows from the upper into the lower chambers on each side before being pumped out of the heart.**

Aorta
is the body's biggest artery.

TO LUNGS

**VALVE 2**
opens to
the lungs.

FROM LUNGS

Upper
left
chamber

**VALVE 3**
opens to
lower left
chamber.

**VALVE 4**
opens to
the aorta.

Lower left
chamber

Lower
right
chamber

ARTERY
TO LOWER
BODY

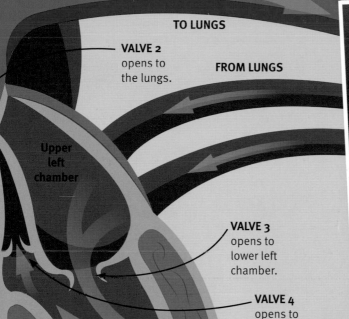

## COUNTING THE BEATS

Some things, such as running and fear, make your heart beat faster. When you sleep, the heart slows down. Otherwise the heart normally beats between 60 and 100 times a minute. You can count your heartbeats by taking your pulse.

▲ *Press your fingers gently against the inside of your wrist and move them until you find your pulse. Use a stopwatch to count how many steady beats you can feel in a minute.*

## ATHLETES HAVE THE BIGGEST HEARTS

Your heart is about the same size as your closed fist, but the heart is a muscle and so exercising your heart makes it stronger and more efficient. Top athletes exercise their hearts so well that their hearts are bigger than normal. This means that they can pump more blood with each beat.

# A drop of blood

**Blood squeezes through the narrowest of capillaries to every part of the body. It carries food and oxygen to every living cell and takes away waste. Each drop of blood contains millions of blood cells floating in a liquid called plasma.**

White blood cells detect and destroy germs. When white cells detect a germ, they trigger the body to make special proteins, called antibodies. Each different type of germ requires a special antibody.

## RED AS BLOOD

Red blood cells collect oxygen from the lungs and transport it to the cells. Your body produces about 2 million new red blood cells every second. All these red blood cells give blood its colour.

**A tiny drop of blood contains about 5 million red blood cells.**

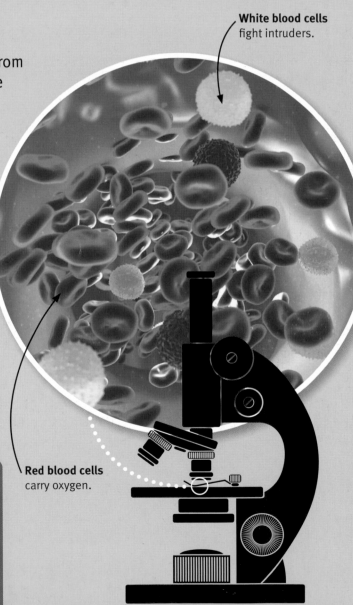

**White blood cells** fight intruders.

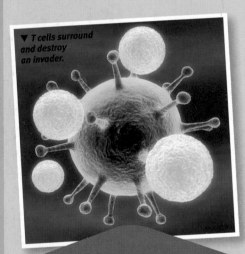

▼ T cells surround and destroy an invader.

**Red blood cells** carry oxygen.

## WARRIOR CELLS

Antibodies lock onto germs but they cannot destroy them. That is the job of white blood cells called T cells. T cells surround the germs and annihilate them.

## PLATELETS TO THE RESCUE

Platelets are blood cells that have the job of stopping bleeding. When capillaries are damaged and bleed, platelets clump together to help the blood to clot and so stop the flow. A clot on the skin dries to form a scab, which protects the wound as new skin grows.

# Cuts and bruises

**31**

**The body has a system to repair damage to the skin and tissues. When the skin is injured, for example by a bump, tiny capillaries under the surface may burst. Blood seeps out, forming a bruise. Major wounds that damage arteries or veins can produce serious bleeding.**

▼ *If a person is badly wounded or loses a lot of blood, they may be given extra blood in a blood transfusion.*

## TRANSFUSION

A transfusion transfers blood from one person to another. There are four main blood groups, O, A, B and AB, and only some of them can be mixed. For example, if your blood is group O, you can only receive group O.

## THE COLOUR OF BRUISES

At first a bruise shows on the skin as a red mark, which soon goes dark blue or purple. Over the next week or two, the bruise fades to yellow as the damage heals.

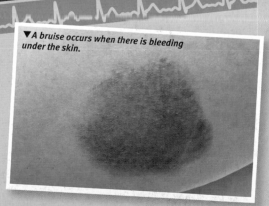

▼*A bruise occurs when there is bleeding under the skin.*

# FOOD AND DIGESTION

The digestive system breaks food down into simple nutrients. These are tiny enough to pass into the blood, which carries them to cells. Digestion starts in the mouth and continues in the stomach and intestines. Solid waste leaves the body through the anus.

## IN THE MOUTH

teeth crunch and chew food while the tongue mixes it with saliva (see page 56).

## OESOPHAGUS

is the tube that joins the throat to the stomach (see page 57).

## STOMACH

churns up food and mixes it with acid to kill germs (see page 58).

## LARGE INTESTINE

absorbs water from undigested food as it moves through on its way to the ANUS (see pages 62–3).

## LIVER

processes digested nutrients and stores some for future use (see page 61).

## SMALL INTESTINE

is where most nutrients are absorbed by the blood (see page 60).

## THE ANUS

is the end of the line for the digestive system, where solid waste leaves the body when you go to the toilet.

**The liver is the biggest gland in the body.**

## FOOD PROCESSOR

The digestive system is a natural food processor. It crushes and grinds food into a soupy mush, which it sprays with digestive juices. These juices break up the food into different nutrients, which slip through the walls of the digestive system into the blood. The rest of the food moves on through the system and leaves the body as waste.

# DIGESTION FACTS

**NARROW INTESTINE**

The small intestine gets its name from being narrow: it is only 2.5 centimetres wide.

**WIDE INTESTINE**

The large intestine is about 7.5 centimetres wide, but is shorter than the small intestine.

**LONG INTESTINES**

Your intestines are about four times as long as you are tall. In adults, this is about 7.5 metres.

**WINDY BACTERIA**

Intestinal gas (breaking wind) is a mixture of gases released by bacteria in the large intestine.

# Necessary nutrients

Nutrients give you energy, keep every part of your body working properly and make you grow. There are four main groups of nutrients – carbohydrates, proteins, fats, and vitamins and minerals. Fibre is not a nutrient, but it makes your digestive system work better. In addition, your body needs lots of water (see pages 68–9).

## CARBOHYDRATES

**What they do:** Give you energy
**Find them in:** Rice, potatoes, bread, pasta and sugars

## PROTEINS

**What they do:** Make new cells and repair and replace old cells
**Find them in:** Fish, meat, eggs, cheese, milk and nuts

## VITAMINS AND MINERALS

**What they do:** Different types of cells need particular vitamins and minerals to work properly
**Find them in:** Vegetables, meat, cereals, cheese and milk

## FATS

**What they do:** Keep you warm and store vitamins A, D and E
**Find them in:** Oils (such as olive oil), milk, cheese, other dairy products and oily fish

## FIBRE

**What it does:** Helps to push food through the intestines and keeps the digestive system healthy
**Find it in:** Vegetables, fruit, wholemeal bread, rice and pasta

## SUPER HEALTHY

All vegetables and fruits are healthy, but some, such as blueberries, broccoli and leafy green vegetables, are super healthy! As well as lots of nutrients, they contain chemicals that can protect against cancer and heart disease.

A healthy diet includes the right amount of each type of nutrient and only a little unhealthy food. No single food contains every type of nutrient, so you need to eat a range of different types of food to be healthy.

**Fruit and vegetables** should be eaten 5 times every day: 3 portions of veg and 2 of fruit.

**Starchy carbohydrates** take longer to digest than sugary ones and supply you with energy for longer.

## FOOD ON THE PLATE

About a third of the food you eat should be starchy CARBOHYDRATES, another third should be fruit and vegetables, and the rest should be dairy foods, fish, chicken, meat and beans.

**The rest** of your diet should be mainly PROTEINS and dairy produce.

Some foods are packed with nutrients, but others are bad for your health.

## HEALTH HAZARDS

Salt, sugar and fat are fine in small amounts, but sweet fizzy drinks and many snacks and ready meals contain unhealthy amounts. Eating too much sugary and fatty food can make a person overweight.

# In the mouth

**Digestion begins in the mouth. Your tongue and lower jaw move food around your mouth while your teeth crush it into smaller pieces. Special glands in your cheeks make saliva, which mixes with the food to make it mushy.**

▼ *Baby teeth (left) usually start to appear in a child's first year. Adult teeth (right) have to last a lifetime!*

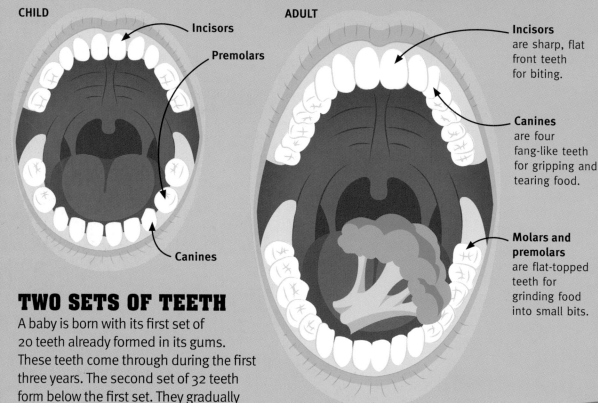

CHILD

Incisors

Premolars

Canines

ADULT

**Incisors**
are sharp, flat front teeth for biting.

**Canines**
are four fang-like teeth for gripping and tearing food.

**Molars and premolars**
are flat-topped teeth for grinding food into small bits.

## TWO SETS OF TEETH

A baby is born with its first set of 20 teeth already formed in its gums. These teeth come through during the first three years. The second set of 32 teeth form below the first set. They gradually push out and replace the baby teeth.

## INSIDE A TOOTH

A tooth is made up of different layers. The outside layer is enamel, the hardest, toughest substance in the body. Below it is dentine, which is similar to bone. At the centre of a tooth is a soft pulp that contains blood and nerves.

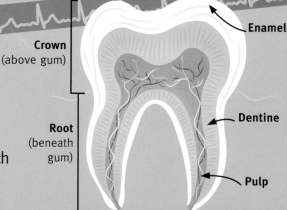

Crown
(above gum)

Root
(beneath gum)

Enamel

Dentine

Pulp

# Don't choke

As soon as a mouthful of food is mushy, your tongue pushes it to the back of your mouth and you swallow automatically. The food moves into your throat and down the oesophagus (foodpipe). A few seconds later, the food reaches your stomach.

## SAFETY FLAP

Two tubes start at the throat — the trachea (windpipe) goes to the lungs, and the OESOPHAGUS goes to the stomach. The EPIGLOTTIS is a special flap in the throat, which closes the trachea when you swallow. This prevents food getting into your lungs and choking you. At the same time, it stops you breathing and speaking while you swallow.

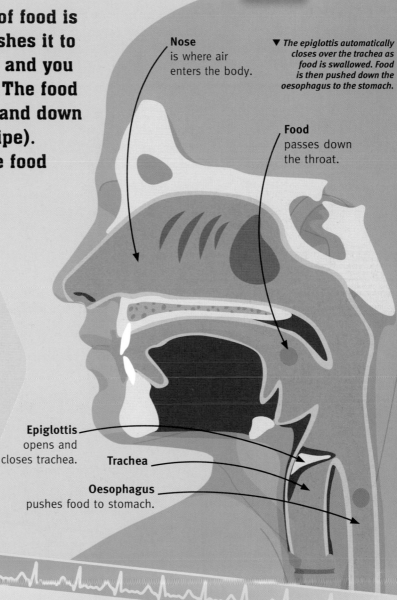

**Nose** is where air enters the body.

▼ *The epiglottis automatically closes over the trachea as food is swallowed. Food is then pushed down the oesophagus to the stomach.*

**Food** passes down the throat.

**Epiglottis** opens and closes trachea.

**Trachea**

**Oesophagus** pushes food to stomach.

## SWALLOWING UPSIDE DOWN

The walls of the oesophagus squeeze and relax to push food to the stomach. This is called peristalsis and works throughout the digestive system. It means that, if you turn upside down as you eat, food will still reach your stomach – but don't try it!

The saliva glands make up to 2 litres (4 glasses) of spit every day.

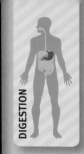

# Stretchy stomach

**The stomach stretches as you eat – an adult stomach can hold 1.5 litres!**

The stomach is a bag with walls made of strong muscles. The walls churn the contents around while acid and juices from the stomach lining get to work. Strong acid kills off most germs and dissolves the food. The stomach works like a food blender, reducing food to a thick soupy liquid called chyme.

## PARDON ME

As the stomach processes food, the food produces gas. Some things, such as fizzy drinks, produce lots of gas, which the stomach needs to get rid of. Then the valve at the top of the stomach opens – and you burp!

**❺ Valve** opens.

### VOMITING VALVE

A valve guards the opening from the oesophagus to the stomach. Most of the time, the valve stops food leaking back into the oesophagus, but it also provides an emergency escape. If you eat something that would make you ill, you vomit. The valve opens and your stomach muscles heave the food out.

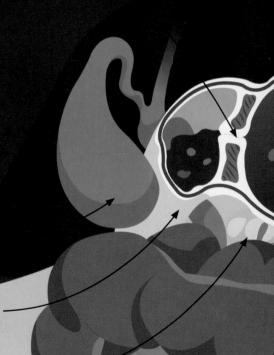

**Liver**

**❻ Gall bladder** stores bile and supplies it to the duodenum.

**❼ Duodenum** receives chyme from the stomach and attacks it with digestive juices.

**❽ Pancreas** supplies alkaline juice to cancel out stomach acid.

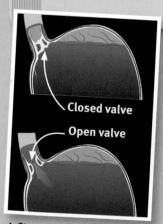

Closed valve

Open valve

▲ Stomach acid deals with most germs in food, but sometimes the stomach needs to get rid of harmful contents by vomiting.

**①Oesophagus** squeezes food down into the stomach.

**②Valve to stomach** opens.

# Juice attack

The stomach releases spurts of soupy chyme through a valve into the small intestine. The first part of the small intestine is called the duodenum. Here chyme is bombarded with digestive juices.

**GREEN GOO**

Juices from the pancreas and liver go into the duodenum. Those from the pancreas are alkaline and so neutralize (cancel out) the acid. Bright-green bile is made in the liver and stored in the gall bladder until it is needed. Like washing-up liquid, bile breaks fat into tiny globules.

**③Stomach** mixes food with acidic juices from the stomach lining.

**④Muscles** in the stomach wall squeeze food.

## MIRACULOUS ENZYMES

ENZYMES are special proteins made in the body to break down food into the tiniest fragments. Cooking uses heat to do something similar, but the amazing thing about enzymes is that they work at normal body temperature. Different types of enzymes break down carbohydrates, proteins and fats.

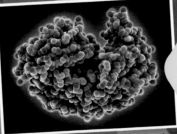

▲ This is a model of a molecule of pepsin. Pepsin is an enzyme that is made in the stomach. It begins the process of breaking up proteins.

Digestive juices contain enzymes, which break nutrients into smaller bits.

# Small intestine

The small intestine is a long tube coiled inside the body. In adults, it is about 6 metres long. Once digestive juices have broken the nutrients into tiny pieces, they are absorbed into the blood.

## HUGE SURFACE

Villi and microvilli massively increase the area of the inside wall of the small intestine. Although each villus is only about 1 millimetre long, it has about 600 even smaller microvilli sticking out from it.

## TAKING IN THE GOODIES

The walls of the small intestine are lined with millions of tiny lumps, like the pile of a carpet. The lumps are called villi and they give a bigger surface through which nutrients can reach the blood. Each villus is covered with even smaller microvilli whose walls are so thin, nutrients pass through them.

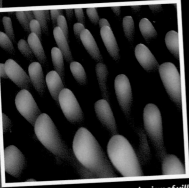

▲ *A microscopic view of villi in the small intestine*

**Each square millimetre of the small intestine is crammed with 10–40 villi.**

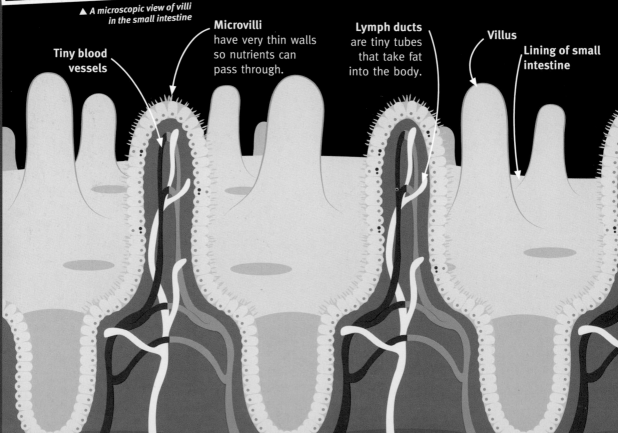

**Tiny blood vessels**

**Microvilli** have very thin walls so nutrients can pass through.

**Lymph ducts** are tiny tubes that take fat into the body.

**Villus**

**Lining of small intestine**

# Multi-tasking liver

 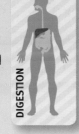

Blood takes nutrients from the small intestine directly to the liver, where they are processed into a form that the body can use. Some of the nutrients are stored here, while the rest are carried to the body in the blood. But the liver also carries out hundreds of other tasks.

## CHEMICAL FACTORY

Here are just some of the jobs the liver does:
- Makes bile (see page 59)
- Controls the amount of sugar in the blood
- Stores energy and some vitamins
- Makes proteins such as antibodies
- Cleans the blood

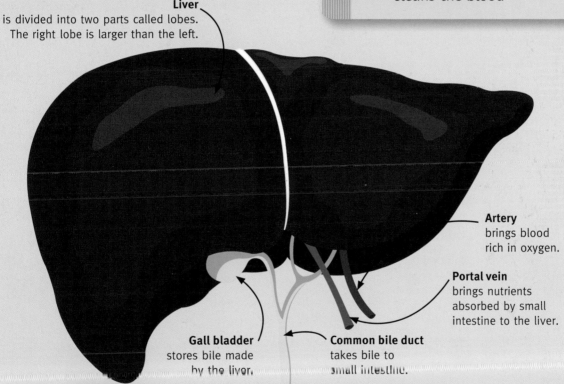

**Liver** is divided into two parts called lobes. The right lobe is larger than the left.

**Artery** brings blood rich in oxygen.

**Portal vein** brings nutrients absorbed by small intestine to the liver.

**Gall bladder** stores bile made by the liver.

**Common bile duct** takes bile to small intestine.

## DESTROYING POISONS

The liver breaks down and removes poisons and waste chemicals in the blood. It destroys alcohol, drugs, pesticides and other poisons, and it removes waste chemicals made in the cells (see page 65). It turns the poisons and waste into UREA, which is processed by the kidneys (see page 66).

You can survive without a stomach, but you cannot survive without your liver.

**41** # Large intestine

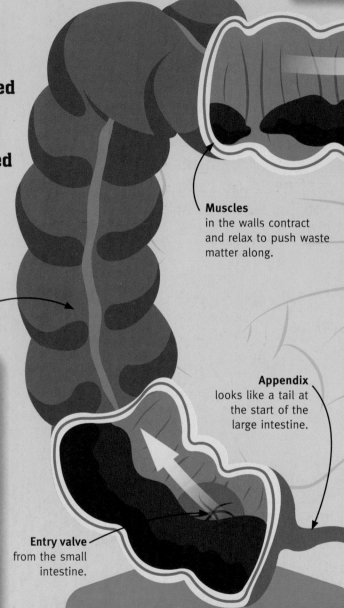

**The large intestine is wrapped around the small intestine.**

A mix of undigested food, water, digestive juices and cells passes into the large intestine (which is also called the colon). It takes up to 20 hours to travel through. On the way, water is absorbed through the intestine walls into the blood, and the remaining paste becomes solid faeces (poo).

**Muscles**
in the walls contract and relax to push waste matter along.

**Ascending colon**
moves food upwards.

**Appendix**
looks like a tail at the start of the large intestine.

**Entry valve**
from the small intestine.

## THE RIGHT BALANCE

Faeces needs to contain enough water to make it soft and easy to push out of the body through the anus. Too much water turns faeces into runny diarrhoea. Too little water makes it hard and difficult to push out. This is called constipation and can be prevented by eating more fibre (see page 54) and drinking plenty of water.

## UNNECESSARY APPENDIX

The appendix is a narrow pocket at the start of the large intestine. It may have once been involved in digestion, but it has no purpose now – although it can cause trouble. Sometimes food blocks the appendix, which becomes infected. This is called appendicitis and is treated by removing the appendix.

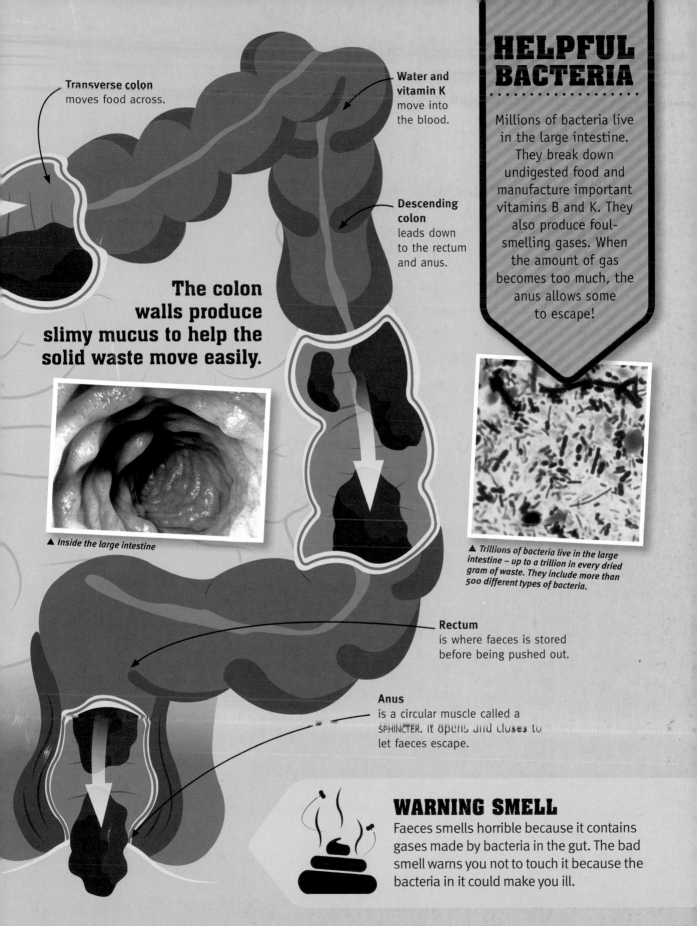

**Transverse colon** moves food across.

**Water and vitamin K** move into the blood.

**Descending colon** leads down to the rectum and anus.

## The colon walls produce slimy mucus to help the solid waste move easily.

▲ Inside the large intestine

▲ *Trillions of bacteria live in the large intestine – up to a trillion in every dried gram of waste. They include more than 500 different types of bacteria.*

**Rectum** is where faeces is stored before being pushed out.

**Anus** is a circular muscle called a SPHINCTER. It opens and closes to let faeces escape.

## WARNING SMELL

Faeces smells horrible because it contains gases made by bacteria in the gut. The bad smell warns you not to touch it because the bacteria in it could make you ill.

# THE URINARY SYSTEM

The kidneys and bladder are the main parts of the urinary system. Kidneys separate out waste and excess water from the blood.

The waste dissolves in water to form urine, which trickles from the kidneys into the bladder.

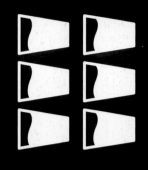

The urinary system produces about 1.5 litres (6 glasses) of urine (wee) a day.

## KIDNEYS

filter blood, removing waste and some water (see page 66).

## BLADDER

stores urine until it becomes uncomfortably full (see page 67).

## URETERS

are the tubes that join the kidneys to the bladder. They are 20 to 25 centimetres long.

the size of a pear, while a full bladder is the size of a grapefruit.

▼ A sample of urine

## WASTE FROM CELLS

Each cell in the body takes oxygen and nutrients from the blood and uses them to make energy. Nutrients include the proteins, vitamins and minerals that cells need to build new cells and carry out their jobs. In the process, cells produce waste, which is collected by the blood and carried to the liver. Here it is turned into urea (see page 66).

## URETHRA

is the tube that takes urine from the bladder and out of the body.

## BLADDER CONTROL

A round muscle called a sphincter keeps the bladder closed. When the muscle relaxes, you wee. A baby cannot control this muscle so it relaxes automatically. It is not until most toddlers are about two years old that they gain control of their bladder.

## URINARY SYSTEM FACTS

### ONE OR TWO?

You have two kidneys but your body can survive for a lifetime with just one.

### YELLOW URINE

Urine is yellow because it contains particles of haemoglobin, the substance that makes blood red.

### LONG URETHRA

A man's urethra is nearly six times longer than a woman's, which is about 4 centimetres long.

### FAST FLOW

If you drink a couple of glasses of water, it takes about an hour for the excess to reach your bladder.

# Busy kidneys

You have two kidneys – one on each side of your back just above the waist. They work hard 24 hours a day, producing urine. The kidneys squeeze excess water out of the blood, and filter out poisons, excess salt and waste products such as urea from the liver.

**Nephrons**
filter waste from blood.

**Vein**
takes filtered blood away.

**Artery**
brings blood in.

## INSIDE A KIDNEY

A kidney has over a million tiny filters, called nephrons. When blood enters a nephron, water is squeezed out along with the nutrients, urea and salts dissolved in it. Only nutrients and as much salt and water as the body needs are reabsorbed. The rest forms urine, which flows down to the bladder.

**Ureter**
carries urine to the bladder.

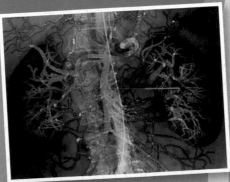

▲ *This scan shows the arteries in red. They are bringing huge amounts of blood to each kidney.*

**TOO SALTY**

Most people eat too much salt. Regularly eating more than a few grams of salt a day can damage the kidneys and cause other serious health problems.

**S**

# Full bladder

As the bladder fills with urine, muscles in its walls stretch until they trigger nerves. The nerves send signals to the brain to relax the muscle around the urethra. The bladder wall contracts and pushes out the urine.

**Ureter** brings urine from the kidneys.

**Bladder** stretches to hold urine.

**Urine** is stored in the bladder.

**Muscles** contract and push urine out when the urethra opens.

**Urethra** is the tube that carries urine to outside the body.

**Circular muscles** contract to hold urethra shut while the bladder fills.

## THE COLOUR OF URINE

The more you drink, the faster your bladder fills up. If you drink a lot, your urine will be dilute and pale yellow. If you are not drinking enough, your urine will be concentrated and dark yellow. Some athletes examine the colour of their urine to make sure they are drinking enough water.

Urine holds: • water • urea • salt • ammonia • yellow remains of red blood cells

An adult bladder holds up to 600 millilitres (2 glasses) of urine comfortably.

# Water in and water out

We cannot survive without water, because our bodies are about 60% water. Blood, saliva and other bodily fluids are mainly water. Cells contain water, too. We constantly lose water, in urine, sweat, faeces and our breath. We replace the lost water by drinking liquids and eating.

## LOST WATER

 **Urine:** Wee is mostly water.

 **Sweat:** You feel sweaty when you are very hot, but you lose water through your skin all the time.

 **Breathing out:** You lose water vapour along with carbon dioxide in the air you breathe out (see page 45).

 **Faeces:** Poo holds water (see page 62).

**Children should drink around 1 to 1.5 litres (6–8 glasses) of water a day, but not all at once!**

## WATER IN FOOD

Most drinks are almost entirely water, but food contains water, too:

| Food | How much is water? |
| --- | --- |
| Cucumber | 95% |
| Most fruit and vegetables | About 80% |
| Potatoes, chicken and fish | 50–70% |
| Bread and cheese | 35–40% |
| Dried fruit | About 15% |

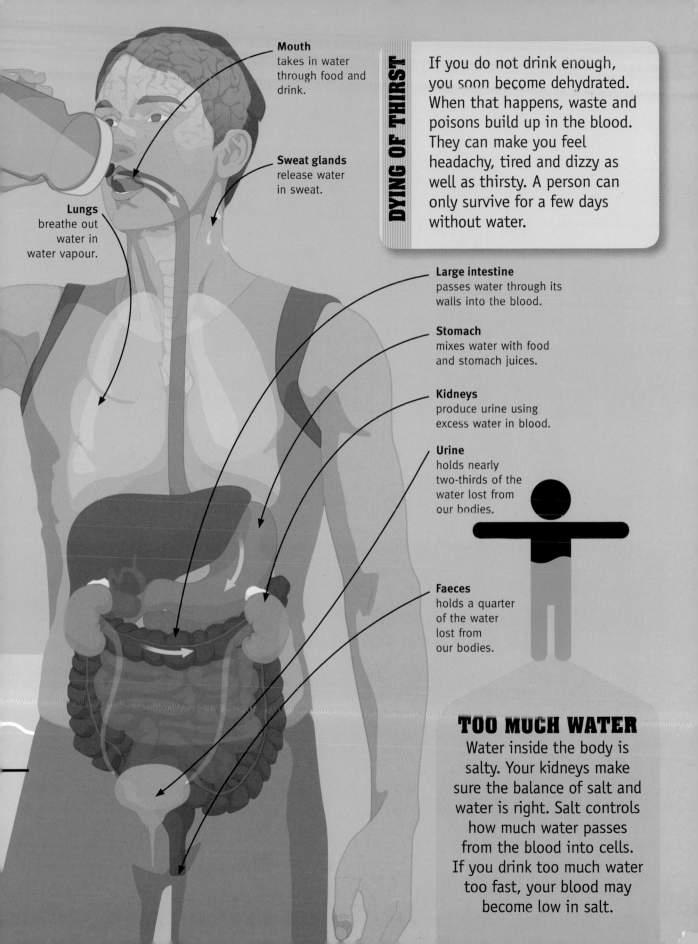

**Mouth**
takes in water through food and drink.

**Sweat glands**
release water in sweat.

**Lungs**
breathe out water in water vapour.

If you do not drink enough, you soon become dehydrated. When that happens, waste and poisons build up in the blood. They can make you feel headachy, tired and dizzy as well as thirsty. A person can only survive for a few days without water.

**Large intestine**
passes water through its walls into the blood.

**Stomach**
mixes water with food and stomach juices.

**Kidneys**
produce urine using excess water in blood.

**Urine**
holds nearly two-thirds of the water lost from our bodies.

**Faeces**
holds a quarter of the water lost from our bodies.

# TOO MUCH WATER
Water inside the body is salty. Your kidneys make sure the balance of salt and water is right. Salt controls how much water passes from the blood into cells. If you drink too much water too fast, your blood may become low in salt.

# CHANGING BODY

Your body grew fastest before you were born.

Every human begins life as a single cell, which divides again and again to form all the trillions of cells in the body! As you grow from a baby into a toddler and then a child, your body changes until, as an adult, you are ready to have children of your own. An adult's body continues to change as they grow older.

**NEWBORN BABY**

A baby is born with every part of their body fully formed, but the baby is helpless. Babies rely on their parents to take care of them, to feed them and to keep them warm, clean and safe.

Hair is longer and thicker than a baby's.

Brain develops the ability to understand facts and ideas.

Child gains control of careful hand movements needed for writing and drawing.

At age two, a toddler is about half their eventual adult height.

Back gradually becomes stronger.

Head is large compared to the rest of the body.

Arms and legs are short compared to the rest of the body.

Legs grow much longer compared to the body.

## BABY

During its first year, a baby becomes bigger and stronger. It cries, smiles and eventually babbles to express how it feels.

## TODDLER

Between one and three years old, toddlers explore the world and start to socialize with other toddlers and family members.

## CHILD

Schoolchildren learn to read, write and understand the wider world through science, history and other subjects.

# An adult is about 20 times heavier than they were at birth. However, a newborn baby is 5,000,000,000 times heavier than the fertilized egg!

Height increases rapidly. By the age of 16–19, most people have almost reached their full height.

Brain cells begin to die from around the age of 25.

Bone mass and height decrease slightly.

Bones and muscles increase in bulk until the late twenties.

Muscles become weaker.

Skin loses elasticity.

Sex organs develop and produce hormones.

Waist increases as fat collects around the abdomen.

## TEENAGER
Older children and teenagers reach PUBERTY, a period during which their bodies slowly become adult (see page 74).

## ADULT
Adults look after themselves and try to contribute to the wider world. They may produce and care for children.

## OLD AGE
Older people may slow down, while hearing, vision and memory may worsen. However, many older people are able to remain active.

# New life

A new life begins when a sex cell (or sperm) from the father joins with a sex cell (or egg) from the mother to form the first cell of a new human being. The first cell divides into two, then four, and so on, to form a ball of cells, which attaches itself to the mother's womb. The cells continue to divide to form all the different parts of the body.

Every person is different from everyone else, unless they are an identical twin.

## CHROMOSOMES

Every human cell contains 46 CHROMOSOMES. When the first cell of a new human being is formed, half its chromosomes come from the father's sperm, while the rest come from the mother's egg. As the first cell divides, its chromosomes are copied again and again.

**1 WEEK**
The first cell divides again and again.

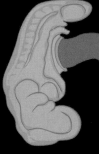

**3–4 WEEKS**
The heart has started beating. Little buds will soon become arms and legs.

**Fingers** have formed.

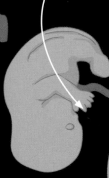

**6–7 WEEKS**
Organs such as brain, kidneys, intestines and liver are starting to function.

**Umbilical cord** supplies food and oxygen.

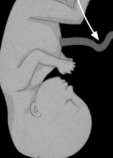

**10–21 WEEKS**
The organs carry on developing. The FOETUS starts to make sucking motions and to hear noises outside the womb.

**Eyelids** can open and close.

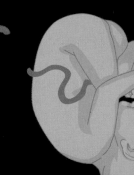

**33–38 WEEKS**
After about 38 weeks in the womb, a fully formed baby is ready to be born.

A cell divides by copying all its chromosomes and then splitting into two cells.

## MALE AND FEMALE CHROMOSOMES

Two chromosomes decide your gender. Mothers always pass on an X chromosome, but fathers can pass on an X or a Y chromosome. If a baby inherits two X chromosomes, it will be a girl. If it gets an X and a Y, it will be a boy.

# Who do you look like?

When a baby is born, family and friends are quick to wonder who the baby looks like. Does he have his mother's eyes? Isn't that her father's nose? The chromosomes that formed your first cell contain genes that decide much about the way you look.

▼ The colour of your hair, skin and eyes are inherited from your parents. Sometimes they are a mixture of both. In this family, which features have these children inherited from each parent?

A human being has between 20,000 and 25,000 different genes.

## WHAT YOU INHERIT

Each chromosome is a bundle of hundreds of genes. Genes are short strips of DNA (deoxyribonucleic acid). DNA contains the instructions for every cell in your body. Genes decide things such as the colour of your hair, the shape of your nose, and how tall you are likely to grow.

Puberty is the time between being a child and an adult. It lasts several years, during which the person's body and emotions change as they get ready to be an adult. It can be an exciting, confusing and difficult time!

## GIRLS' BODIES

For girls, puberty usually begins between the ages of 9 and 13. The ovaries start to release eggs and the womb gets ready to support a baby. The womb lining is formed of cells with a rich blood supply. Once a month, the cells are shed, along with some bleeding. This is called a period.

**Pimples** called acne may form in the skin.

**Breasts** grow larger.

**Hips** become wider.

**Hair grows** under arms and between legs.

**Ovaries** start to release eggs once a month.

**Lining of womb** breaks down once a month.

**Egg** moves down the fallopian tube to womb.

**Monthly blood** leaves body through the vagina.

## HORMONES

Hormones are chemicals that act like messengers in the body. As well as the sex hormones that trigger puberty, the body makes other hormones to perform different tasks. For example, insulin is a hormone that is made in the pancreas and controls the amount of sugar in the blood. Nerves react quickly, but hormones usually work more slowly and over a long period of time.

**Puberty begins when the body produces special chemicals called sex hormones.**

74

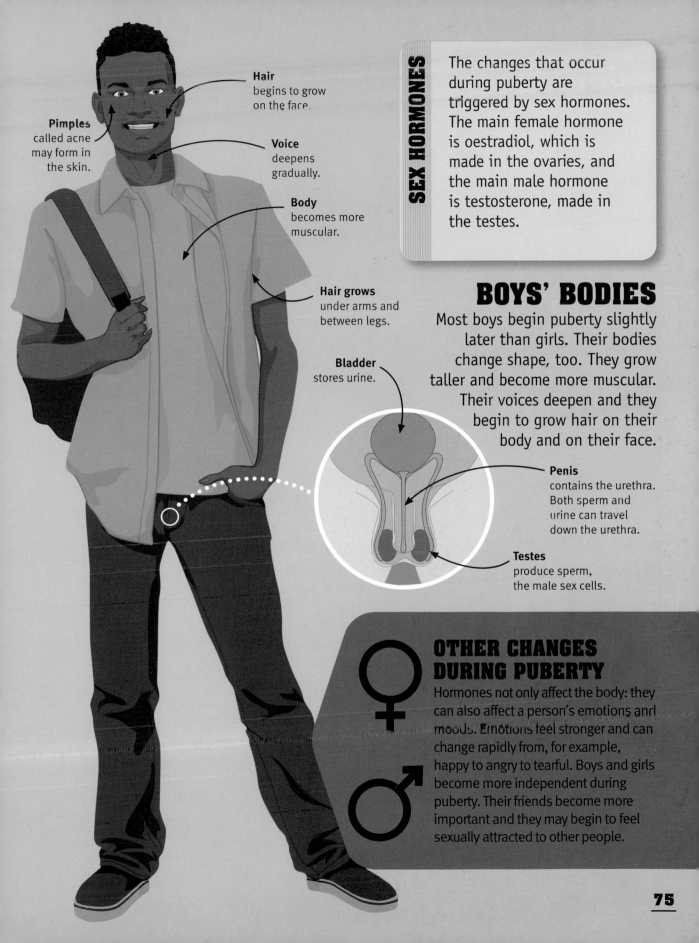

**Hair**
begins to grow on the face.

**Pimples**
called acne may form in the skin.

**Voice**
deepens gradually.

**Body**
becomes more muscular.

**Hair grows**
under arms and between legs.

**Bladder**
stores urine.

# BOYS' BODIES

Most boys begin puberty slightly later than girls. Their bodies change shape, too. They grow taller and become more muscular. Their voices deepen and they begin to grow hair on their body and on their face.

**Penis**
contains the urethra. Both sperm and urine can travel down the urethra.

**Testes**
produce sperm, the male sex cells.

# OTHER CHANGES DURING PUBERTY

Hormones not only affect the body: they can also affect a person's emotions and moods. Emotions feel stronger and can change rapidly from, for example, happy to angry to tearful. Boys and girls become more independent during puberty. Their friends become more important and they may begin to feel sexually attracted to other people.

People continue to change as they grow older. They may move more slowly and find they cannot do all the things they used to do. Most people stop working full-time in their sixties, but the process of ageing actually starts in the mid-twenties.

Grey hair

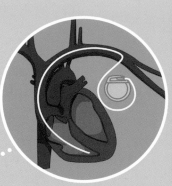

**Pacemaker**
provides electrical pulses to control the heartbeat.

▲ Elderly people can still do adventurous things!

**Skin**
loses its elasticity and forms wrinkles.

**Hip joint**
replaced by an artificial joint when the cartilage has worn away.

## BIONIC GRANDPARENTS

Doctors and scientists have invented ways of replacing or improving parts of the body. They include:

**False teeth**

**Artificial hip and knee joints**

**Hearing aids**

**Pacemakers that control the heartbeat**

**Hearing aid** can be clipped onto the ear or worn inside the ear canal.

## WHAT'S THAT YOU SAY?

Older people often find it harder to catch what people are saying. This is because their ears no longer pick up the full range of human sounds, so words are muffled.

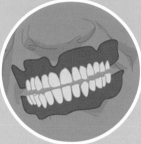

**False teeth** can be inserted into the bone or held in place by a plastic bridge.

## SLOWING DOWN

By the age of 70 or 80, most people have become much slower. Their cells take longer to repair themselves and their organs may not work so well. Their bones may become more brittle, and joints may become stiffer and more painful. The brain also slows down. It may take longer for older people to think and remember things, particularly things that happened more recently.

**Knee joint** can be replaced if cartilage wears away.

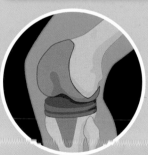

## Elderly people often find the distant past easier to remember than recent events.

## LIVING LONGER

More people are staying healthy and living longer than in the past. The number of people over 100 years of age is increasing, and some live beyond 110 years. The increase in life span is due mainly to advances in medicine and healthier lifestyles.

# GLOSSARY

**AEROBIC EXERCISE**
Exercise that makes
the heart and lungs
work harder.

**AIR SAC**
A tiny 'balloon' in the lungs
which takes in oxygen from
the air and releases carbon
dioxide from the blood.

**ALLERGY**
When the body reacts to
something as though it
were harmful, although it is
not harmful to most people.

**ANUS**
The sphincter muscle at the
end of the large intestine,
where solid waste leaves
the body.

**ARTERY**
Blood vessel that carries
blood away from the heart.

**BLOOD VESSEL**
A tube that carries
blood. Arteries, veins
and capillaries are all
blood vessels.

**BRONCHIAL TUBES**
Tubes that branch off the
trachea and carry air deep
into and out of the lungs.

**BRONCHIOLE**
A narrow tube that reaches
deep inside the lung to the
air sacs.

**CAPILLARY**
A narrow blood vessel,
which takes blood to and
from the cells.

**CARBOHYDRATE**
Sugar and starch in food
that the body uses to
get energy.

**CARTILAGE**
A strong, bendy substance,
which forms at the end
of bones.

**CELL**
A cell is the building block
of life. All types of living
things are made of cells.

**CHROMOSOME**
A bundle of genes, each of
which is a short strip of DNA.

**DNA (DEOXYRIBONUCLEIC
ACID)**
DNA is a complex molecule
that contains the
instructions for every cell
in the body.

**ENZYMES**
Special proteins that take
part in chemical changes in
the body, including
breaking down food.

**EPIGLOTTIS**
A flap at the back of
the throat that closes the
trachea when you swallow
food or liquid.

**FIBRES**
Threads of muscle; tough
parts of plants that cannot
be digested.

**FOETUS**
A baby before it is born.

**FUNGUS**
A form of life that
includes mushrooms,
yeast and moulds. Some
fungi can cause diseases,
such as athlete's foot
and ringworm.

**GLAND**
A part of the body that
produces useful substances,
such as sweat, digestive
juices or hormones.

**INTESTINES**
The long tube that
connects your stomach to
your anus (bottom).

**JOINT**
Place where bones meet
each other. Some joints
allow the bones to move
relative to each other.

**KERATIN**
A hard substance from
which hair, nails and
the outer layer of skin
are made.

**LIGAMENT**
A band of gristle which
holds a joint together.